A PRACTICAL GUIDE TO
OVERCOMING OVERPARENTING

PARENT OR PARTNER

IN FAVOR OF
VIBRANT MARRIAGES
& HEALTHY KIDS

SALLY LIVINGSTON, LMFT

Parent or Partner © 2023 by Sally Livingston. All rights reserved.

Printed in the United States of America

Published by Reachout Publishing
PO Box 159, Clyde, AB T0G 0P0
www.reachloveconnect.com

All rights reserved. This book contains material protected under International and Federal Copyright Laws and Treaties. Any unauthorized reprint or use of this material is prohibited. No part of this book may be reproduced or transmitted in any form or by any means, electronic or mechanical, including photocopying, recording, or by any information storage and retrieval system, without express written permission from the author.

Identifiers:
ISBN: 978-1-7387721-4-8 (paperback)
ISBN: 978-1-7387721-6-2 (ebook)

Available in paperback, e-book, and audiobook

Although the author and publisher have made every effort to ensure that the information in this book was correct at press time, the author and publisher do not assume and hereby disclaim any liability to any party for any loss, damage, or disruption caused by errors or omissions, whether such errors or omissions result from negligence, accident, or any other cause. Some names and identifying details have been changed to protect the privacy of individuals […]"

Excerpt From
Parent or Partner
Sally Livingston
This material may be protected by copyright.

- "ENGLISH STANDARD VERSION ® Copyright© 2001 by Crossway, a publishing ministry of Good News Publishers. Used with permission.
- Scriptures marked NKJV are taken from the NEW KING JAMES VERSION (NKJV): Scripture taken from the NEW KING JAMES VERSION®. Copyright© 1982 by Thomas Nelson, Inc. Used by permission. All rights reserved.
- Scriptures marked HCSB are taken from the HOLMAN CHRISTIAN STANDARD BIBLE (HCSB): Scripture taken from the HOLMAN CHRISTIAN STANDARD BIBLE, copyright© 1999, 2000, 2002, 2003 by Holman Bible Publishers, Nashville Tennessee. All rights reserved.
- Scriptures marked THE VOICE are taken from THE VOICE (The Voice): Scripture taken from THE VOICE ™. Copyright© 2008 by Ecclesia Bible Society. Used with permission. All rights reserved.
- "Scripture taken from the NEW AMERICAN STANDARD BIBLE®, Copyright © 1960,1962,1963,1968,1971,1972,1973,1975,1977,1995 by The Lockman Foundation. Used by permission."
- The Holy Bible, English Standard Version® (ESV®) Copyright © 2001 by Crossway, a publishing ministry of Good News Publishers. All rights reserved.
- New Revised Standard Version Bible, copyright 1989, Division of Christian Education of the National Council of the Churches of Christ in the United States of America. Used with permission. All rights reserved.
- New English Translation (NET) NET Bible® copyright ©1996-2006 by Biblical Studies Press, L.L.C. http://netbible.com All […]"

Excerpt From
Parent or Partner
Sally Livingston
This material may be protected by copyright.

Dedication

Above all, I thank you, God for your unfailing love. I can do nothing apart from You and all things through You!

To my sweetheart of 32 years, Scott. Thank you for loving me and making me a wife and mother. This book is a testament to your support and our partnership.

To my adult children – Leah, Andrew, and Sarah – I am blessed beyond measure to be your mother. Thank you for the inspiration and encouragement you are to me.

Table of Contents

INTRODUCTION

ONE
The Balancing Act 1

TWO
The Pressure to Overparent 7

THREE
The Chicken or The Egg? 17

FOUR
Tethered or Vacated? 23

FIVE
Which Comes Last? 33

INTRODUCTION

I'm so excited that you're here. I've been praying for you! In the months leading up to the release of *Parent or Partner*, I have been going to different cities, speaking to groups of people, and asking the question at the heart of this book, *"which comes first?"* The response has been overwhelming. I have seen first-hand a deep hunger to find a way to stay connected and vibrant in marriage while at the same time raising great kids. I know you, like these audiences, want to be both a great parent and a great partner; that's most likely why you are reading this now. The struggle is real; you are not imagining it. The cultural pull toward a focus on being a parent over being a partner is growing more strongly every day.

I am passionate about helping people experience vibrancy in their marriages. I also love working to help parents understand their role and enjoy the ride that is parenting. I have worked toward both ends for almost 30 years and have been blessed to walk this journey with so many people. I hope this little book brings some practical help to you in balancing the roles of being a spouse and a parent.

I pray that you will find inspiration, motivation, encouragement, and comfort on the following pages as you read them and the courage to change your focus if it is not where it needs to be. Take your time; though this book is small, the impact can be BIG!

PARENT OR PARTNER QUIZ

PARENT OR PARTNER

WHAT IS YOUR ROLE FOCUS?

	Yes	No
1 Do your conversations with your spouse mostly revolve around the kids?	☐	☐
2 Do you look forward to time alone with your spouse?	☐	☐
3 Do you feel overwhelmed by your kids' activities?	☐	☐
4 Is physical intimacy with your spouse a priority for you?	☐	☐
5 Do you find it hard to say no when it comes to your children?	☐	☐
6 Do you have a daily check-in with your spouse?	☐	☐
7 Do you do things for your children they can/should do for themselves?	☐	☐

	Yes	No
8. Do you spend time with your spouse away from the kids regularly?	☐	☐
9. Are you usually thinking about your kids?	☐	☐
10. Do you share dreams with your spouse?	☐	☐
11. Do you and your spouse have a parenting plan?	☐	☐
12. Did your parents have a good marriage?	☐	☐
13. Do you plan ahead for time with your spouse?	☐	☐
14. Do you and your spouse argue frequently about the kids or how to parent them?	☐	☐
15. Do you know your spouse's current stressors?	☐	☐
16. Do you find it easier to talk to your kids than to your spouse?	☐	☐

PARENT OR PARTNER

WHAT IS YOUR ROLE FOCUS?

SCORING KEY:

GIVE YOURSELF 2 POINTS FOR A <u>YES</u> ANSWER TO THESE QUESTIONS:

1,3,5,7,9,11,14,16

GIVE YOURSELF 2 POINTS FOR A <u>NO</u> ANSWER TO THESE QUESTIONS:

2,4,6,8,10,12,13,15

ADD UP YOUR TOTAL POINTS TO GET YOUR RFS (ROLE FOCUS SCORE) BETWEEN 0-32

A score of 2-16 indicates a Partner focus
A score of 16-32 indicates a Parent focus

ONE
The Balancing Act

The most important work you will ever do will be within the walls of your own home.
—Harold B. Lee

Balance is not something you find; it's something you create.
—Jana Kingsford

Life is full of balancing acts! A series of choices to be made between essential things. It seems we are constantly trying to find that center point to balance all the differing elements. Because life is constantly changing, we are consistently faced with choices that seem to be opposing. What starts as a balancing effort can easily become an either/or proposition. It becomes more like a seesaw; if one side is up, the other is automatically down. That's a fallacy of thinking that contributes to the belief that you must choose one or the other, or one *over* the other. It is especially hard when the choice is between two equally important things like your marriage relationship and your kids. Because both are highly valued, it would be logical to assume that balance looks like a scale with both sides being weighted equally as the goal. This is not the case. The balancing act between being a partner and a parent is neither a seesaw – either/or – nor a scale that is to be weighted equally. The type of balance needed here is more like the balance required to roll a log or drive a Segway. Have you ever done either one of those activities? If you haven't experienced it firsthand, have you seen someone trying to roll a log or drive a Segway? The key is the ability of the person rolling or driving to maintain a balanced state. That ability determines the motion forward; it determines the success of the endeavor. The balance to be achieved in the choice of parent or partner is like this – it is rank ordered. Balance in the first creates balance in the second.

With this in mind, we start with that balancing question. Are you a parent or a partner? You are likely both of those if you are reading this book. If you are, this is not a seesaw question but a focus question. So, let's get more focused and ask it this way. Are you a parent-partner? Or are you a partner-parent? Perhaps you are wondering what the difference is between the two. At face value, they are interchangeable, but the delineation of the two questions lies in word placement. The word that comes first in each question indicates the focus. What is focused on will become emphasized and will become the engine to drive both roles. So now that we realize it is not an either/or proposition, one question remains: "Which comes first?"

A study on marital satisfaction following the transition to

parenting shows that the highest level of marital satisfaction for a couple is on the day of their wedding, after which follows a generally slow but steady decline. And statistically, if you have children, that satisfaction decreases twice as fast as if you don't have children. At least 15 long-term studies agree with the premise of declining satisfaction after becoming parents. More pointedly, the research indicates that the lowest point of marital satisfaction is after the birth of the first child. Additional layers of stress are added with the birth of each subsequent child. Clearly, there is a significant relationship between marital satisfaction and having children.

> *"Our findings are in line with other research, which showed that the number of children can be considered as a global, negative correlate of marital satisfaction. Several theories that motivate marital satisfaction research provide rationale to the expectation that as the family (i.e., number of children) grows, the relationship between spouses is being challenged." (Kowal, 2021, page 2021)*

This would explain some book and article titles that are currently out on the topic. Here is a sample of what a current search pulls up from the Wall Street Journal, Jancee Dunn, and the Washington Post, respectively:

> "Here Comes Baby, There Goes the Marriage."
> "How Not to Hate Your Husband After Kids."
> "Why Having Children is Bad for Your Marriage. (But It's Usually Worth It)"

PARENT OR PARTNER

In an article from the National Journal of Medicine titled, *"Attachment, Marital Satisfaction, and Divorce During the First Fifteen Years of Parenthood,"* the authors state the following:

> *"The birth of a first child presents a significant challenge for married couples, as their relationship undergoes a transition from a dyadic unit to a family of three or more. This transition may affect the family system in many different ways, both positive and negative. On the positive side, parents often experience a sense of gratification and joy over having a new baby. On the negative side, they may also experience exhaustion, lack of time for themselves, and more disagreement over issues pertaining to care of the baby and the division of family labor. These strains and difficulties may affect the quality of their relationship as a couple adversely." (e.g.,* Belsky & Pensky, 1988; Cowan & Cowan, 2000; Twenge, Campbell, & Foster, 2003*).*

This tension is not new or surprising. The move from couple to parent can be fast and furious, with little time for adjustment. Which am I supposed to give more to? How can I do both well in my exhaustion? How do I respond in a balanced way when one takes up all my time and energy? Clearly, the demands of an infant require focused attention and set the stage for the shift toward the imbalance in roles. It is a shock to the system, no matter the level of preparation for the child, to go from friends and lovers in the honeymoon stage to exhausted parents struggling just to get some sleep. The couple once focused on *sexy time* morphs into parents entrenched in perpetual *messy time* in one fell swoop. It is a season where nothing is private, nothing is clean (for long), and nothing is the same anymore.

Balancing the focus in the first few years of parenthood is challenging, and the needs of the infant win the early *battles*. If the couple is not aware and awake, the *war* will also be won by attrition, and parenting the children will become the couple's focus and emphasis going forward. This sets the couple up for the trap that is overparenting. In the next chapter, we will look at the pressures to overparent and the resulting problems.

PARENT OR PARTNER

TWO
The Pressure to Overparent

The goal of parenting isn't to create perfect kids. It's to point our kids to the perfect God.

—*Lindsey Bell*

It is not what you do for your children but what you have taught them to do for themselves that will make them successful human beings.

—*Ann Landers*

Don't handicap your children by making their lives easy.
—*Robert A. Heinlein*

Kids who never have any accountability for their actions will continue through life thinking nothing is their fault, and everything is owed to them.

—*Dr. Laura*

More than ever, our culture seems to be sending the message to parents that they need to *do* everything and *be* everything so their kids can have everything. Additionally, they are to have it all at once and right now, without trying, without struggling, without experiencing any pain or any problem along the way. This cultural pressure has become extreme. Comparison is a common trap because of those perfectly curated Instagram posts depicting other parents producing the perfect offspring with ease. Though we can know this is not reality, the illusion is strong when scrolling through the feed. The once common approach to letting your children develop and explore as they grow has been hijacked by the idea that parents are responsible for building into them everything they need to win in life. Parents feel the weight of this faulty notion that they are responsible for their children's intellect, talent, confidence, and personality. Dr. Russell Barkley, a clinical psychologist and internationally renowned authority on ADHD, speaks to this belief. He calls it "the Mozart effect" - the belief that if enough classical music is played to children in utero, genius can be ushered in where it was not present otherwise. He discusses the idea that parents are overwhelmed and set into panic by the belief that they can "engineer or design" their children and that it is their responsibility to do so.

If accepted as truth, this belief increases the pressure on parents and strains the tension between parenting and partnering. Parenting, as a result, becomes a competitive sport. It becomes about access, achievement, and accomplishment in an attempt to create the best opportunities and environment for the child to "win." It fosters comparison and anxiety. The problem with this competitive agenda is that both parent and child end up losing.

THE PRESSURE TO OVERPARENT

There are some updated terms for this focus on parenting that I discovered as I was preparing to speak to audiences that I found very interesting. They're a little bit less direct than the descriptors used some years before, perhaps they are a bit more PC, but they're actually hard-hitting regarding the impact on children.

Try these on for size:
- overparenting
- overly concerned parenting
- over present parents (that's the *helicopter parent* renamed)
- over nurturing parents
- overindulgent parents

Do you see a theme here? The common denominator is the word *over* – meaning too much. Do you fall into any of those descriptions? Find yourself doing too much? You are not alone! Being stressed out, frazzled, and run ragged as parents are badges of honor worn on the sleeve of so many. Are you wearing that badge today? Are you stressed out? Are you frazzled? Are you frantic? Stress levels are an easy conversation starter – everyone can participate. Parent stress is not new – but it seems parents are stressed out exponentially more today. It makes sense that coping mechanisms and strategies are used to deal with parent burnout. Riding the line of burnout or redlining and hoping to hold it all together *is* a strategy, but not a great one. Another of the strategies used is to *divide and conquer*. "You take Susie to ballet; I'll take Johnny to baseball. Then we'll swap cars because I need the bigger car to take the dog to the vet, and then we will meet up again for the hand-off for you to drive Johnny to his *second* round of baseball practice. Then I'll take Susie home to get dinner and homework started, and we will help Johnny with his when he gets home. Oh, and feed him somewhere in between!" Whew! You know, dividing and conquering is an everyday occurrence in many households. Another coping tactic is *ships passing in the night*. You work in shifts. "You take the night shift; I'll take the day shift." Maybe you will see one another in passing, but if so, it is brief, and possibly one of you is not awake. One of the more common strategies is the old standby, "We'll just put our marriage on hold while we parent. See you in 15-18 years! We'll get back to *us* once the job is done. We have to focus on the kids for the sake of the kids." No wonder we experience our marriages as *divided, passed over,* and *on hold.*

It is what we do to manage the imbalance of overparenting, and we may not even perceive it to be a problem. How could sacrificing for your children be wrong when it sounds and feels so right? Unfortunately, what you may be sacrificing for the kids to have it all, is your marriage. The seesaw approach to balance takes effect with these coping mechanisms. It's either the kids or the marriage.

There are very real problems with overparenting beyond the toll it takes on the marriage. It also takes a toll on the children as they grow into adulthood. When the parent is overly involved, these are some common outcomes for your child:

Helplessness – Children who are constantly helped or micromanaged, though they are not actually helpless, reach a point where they don't try because they have never exercised that muscle – this is called *learned helplessness*. If someone is always doing everything for them, the message comes across as "you *can't* do it; why try."

Irresponsibility – If children have never borne the weight of their choices – they don't ever have the opportunity to learn responsibility. This can create a demanding and insecure child who becomes a demanding and insecure adult.

Entitlement – When things come to a child without a cost, they develop unreasonable expectations. The child develops magical thinking related to how things come to them. Immediate gratification is expected – the instant access world they live in ensures that. Parents feel upset when their children have such unreasonable expectations – but forget who and what set that high bar.

Personal and Professional Difficulties – When a child doesn't have to work through relational struggles, they don't have experience with conflict and the knowledge that it is normal and inevitable. They end up fearing or avoiding it and struggle relationally at home and eventually at work.

Poor problem resolution – If the parent swoops in whenever there is a problem for a child to solve or tells their child how to do it, they are unprepared for a world with any problems.

Children will face problems, and the best way to prepare them to deal healthily is to allow them to practice problem-solving in the safest place. That is at home with their parents guiding and encouraging them.

Lack of self-control – Children who are not required to control their behaviors or who get mixed messages and inconsistency from their parents are less likely to develop self-control. Self-control is developed experientially over time. The goal of parental discipline is to teach the child self-discipline.

Anxiety and fear – Overparenting stems from the anxiety a parent feels; anxiety is wrapped up in fear. Children, like sponges, soak that in. They are likely to mimic the emotional atmosphere of the home, especially in the creation of their own marriage and family.

Lack of confidence – When the parent is the reason a child has confidence, they will never develop their own. They can only borrow the parent's confidence for so long.

In addition to this list, we can add depression and unhealthy thinking, financial issues, lack of spiritual connection, parenting problems as adults, materialism, and externalization of value.

According to a Journal of Family and Consumer Sciences Education article, overindulging children is "giving them too much of what looks good too soon and for too long and giving them things or experiences that are inappropriate for their age, interests, or talents. It is the process of giving things to children to meet the adult's needs, not the child's."

That's a dagger in the heart. Haven't we all, at one time or another, met our needs in a way that was less appropriate for our child? At a low level, giving a child a lollipop to stop them from crying or having a meltdown is a form of this. But the term *overindulging* has more meat on its bones. It might be more like giving a child a handheld computer (known as a cellphone) with access to the internet and all that comes with it before they are ready to handle it - so we can know they are safe and reach them whenever we want to or need to. We sit them in front of that same screen at dinners in public, so they won't make a scene. We then install monitoring capacity and read everything they send out on this *necessary* device because they are too young to know the ramifications of a comment or photo that will never be lived down or erased.

Someone wrote that the cell phone is the *world's longest umbilical cord*. We're always connected to our kids in a way that doesn't allow or encourage them to be apart from us. Believe it or not, when I was a child, and even when my children were in elementary school, there was no such thing. When I dropped them off, I knew nothing about their day until the drive-time conversations on the way home. Parents now feel like they need to know where their children are all the time and are having text conversations with them while they are in school about things they can and perhaps should be handling on their own. Overparenting gets in the way of children being able to master their needed developmental tasks and form learning necessary life lessons. Lest you think I'm naïve and "judgy" about this generation of parents – please hear me – my generation also had our conveniences and made similar choices that served our needs over the needs of the children. Yes, I confess, I did it too! Unfortunately, for today's parents, the results may have a heftier price tag.

What does it look like to overparent or overindulge children? As mentioned before, it can look like giving too much or taking over and doing things for our children instead of helping them learn to do those things for themselves. It can also be a result of what is referred to as soft structures. It is exactly what it sounds like – soft and fuzzy lines instead of clear and firm ones. This would include setting rules but not enforcing them, excusing behaviors that are unacceptable, and a lack of follow-through with what is said to the child. Basically, it teaches the child that you are not credible – that what you say is not true and does not hold any weight. One of the greatest things you can give your child is consistency and structure. They need to be able to see that your words and behaviors line up so they can trust you and ultimately respect the boundaries of others and hold them for themselves.

If you have ever heard me speak or have been a client, you may have heard me say this more than once … your child needs to know sooner rather than later that *their world is their problem to solve*. If they think it's your problem, they will let you solve it.

THE PRESSURE TO OVERPARENT

If *you* think their problems are yours, you will teach them they are right in very short order. But if you let them know that their world is their problem to solve, you are teaching them that they can solve the issues that are presented. They gain confidence from trying, and even failing, they learn not to fear but to lean in and move forward. What does this look like practically? It is a stepped-back position – one that respects your child as a separate entity from you. This vantage point allows you to see that their behaviors and choices are theirs, as are the consequences of those behaviors and choices. It is offering a cool, calm, and collected demeanor in front of the child, saving the meltdowns and breakdowns for your closet once you are alone. It allows you to be less emotionally involved and not take their daily choices personally. This positioning helps them learn to carry the weight instead of waiting for you to fix things. Of course, all of this must be done in line with their age and developmental stage. The main goal is for you, the parent, to gradually back out of the active *parenting* role while focusing on the longer-term relationship. Influence is the outcome of this formula. You will have influence with them, and they will seek your guidance. This transfer of power and responsibility is ongoing until you are in the "trusted advisor" seat of an adult-to-adult relationship with someone who happens to be your child. (See diagram on page 62.)

This is a tough chapter, and maybe you are feeling a bit discouraged at this point. You might be realizing some of your current focus leads you to overparent. The incredibly good news is that you can shift this pretty quickly. With insight, change is possible.

PARENT OR PARTNER

Keep reading, and you'll get some practical help in a couple of chapters! Hold on!

THREE
The Chicken or The Egg?

It is not a lack of love, but a lack of friendship that makes unhappy marriages.

—*Friedrich Nietzsche*

The most important thing a father can do for his children is to love their mother.

—*Theodore Hesburgh*

As to the question at hand, Parent or Partner, is there a specific formula? How much time, attention, and energy am I supposed to give to my husband? How much am I to give my kids? Is there a direct answer out there? As a Christian, I look to the Bible to find answers. In this case, I don't find the specific parent or partner formula spelled out – wouldn't it be great if it were that easy? But we are not left to wonder. When we don't see answers spelled out specifically in the Bible, we can look at what is shown through behaviors and actions. This takes me back to the question, "Which comes first?"

PARENT OR PARTNER

Have you ever grappled with the chicken or the egg riddle, and which came first? It can drive you crazy! Is there actually an answer? It seems to be a circular exercise that lands nowhere. It goes like this, "Which came first, the chicken or the egg?" Well, of course, the chicken comes first because a chicken is required for an egg to exist. But wait, the chicken comes from the egg. Okay, then the egg comes first. But what laid the egg? The chicken did! Do you see what I mean? It's frustrating!

In the question at hand, we are fortunate that we don't have to go round and round, landing nowhere. In the first book of the Bible, we read the creation story. Although we don't find that precise formula, there is a definitive answer. The answer is clear; the 'chicken' came first. In fact, there were no 'eggs,' only 'chickens' – and it was one 'chicken' at a time.

Okay, we can stop talking about our fine feathered friends now and move past the analogy. First, God created Adam and then Eve from Adam's rib. In another definitive statement, God shows us with action His intentions. The very first act recorded in the Bible with those first two people was marriage. Why was this the first thing? To put it simply, God gave us His take on the importance He places on marriage. First things were done first. He married them as a model for us, a symbol of His covenant to us, His presence with us, and the marriage of Christ with His church. It was also a clear message about marriage and its importance in God's plan for humanity. That is how important marriage is; it was first - it *is* first. Here we see that God reveals the answer to the question, and there is no contest! After this, Adam and Eve had their little 'eggs' and completed the loop for the birth of the riddle that would frustrate us for years to come. The first couple became the first parents, and it looks like they, too, had some problems with the two roles based on the outcome. If you want to read that story in Genesis, it's a very interesting family drama.

We can look to a couple of additional verses in the Bible to see what God says about marriage and parenting. Let's start with this verse on marriage. Hebrews 13:4 says it directly.

> "Marriage should be honored by all."

I don't believe we do that very well today in our society; it's certainly not easy to do in the face of what seems to be a war against marriage. If you try to honor marriage today and the Biblical definition, you are labeled and derided. In fact, many studies show record low marriage rates, revealing its demise as an institution and hinting that married people may become the minority. All of this is trending despite the clear data that being married has tremendous benefits. The Heritage Foundation, in an article titled, "Why the Declining Marriage Rate Affects Everyone" reports:

Decades of statistics have shown that, on average, married couples have better physical health, more financial stability, and greater social mobility than unmarried people.

Other studies show that the children of those couples are more likely to experience higher academic performance, emotional maturity, and financial stability than children who don't have both parents in the home.

Unfortunately, the downward slide is the course we are on; unless we change things in our culture, our children will face a vastly different world. God's Word gives the antidote, and it bears repeating; *marriage should be honored by all.*

Let's look at a verse about parenting. Proverbs 22:6 (MSG) says,

"Train up a child in the way he should go, and when he is old, he will not get lost."

I like the Message version of that verse. The idea that what we seed and sow into our children at the earliest stages will keep them from getting lost later in life is so important. A key concept in this verse is one of the smallest words, *go*. Your children are going to go. They are *supposed* to go, and if you don't want them to go and try to hold them back from going, you will have a tough time parenting, especially in the teenage years. Train them – or raise them - in the way they should go suggests the inclusion of a *go plan*. Prepare knowing they're going to go - be okay that they're going and help them go! Help them instead of holding them back, and everyone will be much happier and healthier.

Another important concept in this verse is the fuller phrase that contains the word, go. The phrase is *'in the way he should go.'* The Hebrew meaning for this refers to a child's uniqueness or the way God 'bent' them – their desires, passions, and personality. Too often, we train them in the way *we* think they should go instead of how they are bent by God. Our job as parents is not to see them through our lens and try to bend them in a way that is easier, more satisfying, or acceptable for us. It is not to change them to meet the cultural definition of success. In stark contrast, our role is more of a shepherd to guide and direct. This can be difficult to refrain from the urge to overparent but instead help them find their interests, desires, and passions. Our role is to help them understand how God wired them and pursue their dreams. For many parents, this can feel out of control and not sufficient to meet the demands of today's world. The shepherd's role, however, can be misperceived. The Bible gives us a great picture of how the shepherd is to care for his sheep in Psalm 23. It is an especially significant role. In fact, it is crucial. As shepherds, parents have an essential responsibility of choosing the fields our 'sheep' graze in and the direction in which they go. The goal is to keep them safe and fed along the way and corral them when they wander off as sheep will do. It is to lead them through the difficult valleys toward the determined destination. The goal of the shepherd is *not*, however, to turn a sheep into a goat. Parents are to help their children make better decisions and choices as they grow with an understanding of themselves in relation to God, their permanent parent.

How can we do this? We need help. We need God's help first and foremost to resist the urge to overparent and forego the necessary focus on our marriage. In the next chapter, I will illustrate a couple of options that may help you make some new choices.

FOUR
Tethered or Vacated?

The real act of marriage takes place in the heart, not in the ballroom or church or synagogue. It's a choice you make on your wedding day, and over and over again, and that choice is reflected in the way you treat your husband.

—Barbara De Angelis

I have no way of knowing whether or not you married the wrong person. But I do know that if you treat the wrong person like the right person, you could well end up having married the right person after all. It is far more important to BE the right kind of person than it is to marry the right person.

—Zig Ziglar

God's design for the family began with Adam and Eve in the Garden. He started with the married couple – the dyad - in connection with Him. From there, He ordered the focus, knowing that the marriage relationship is primary and that the children are the recipients of whatever is happening there.

In marital therapy, one of the tools we use to diagram the family is called a genogram. Murray Bowen developed this tool as a graphic representation of family members and generational patterns. It is helpful for what we will be discussing in this chapter to have a visual tool from which to work, so I have created this for your reference. (See diagram on page 28)

In a Christian marriage, God is the head, and the husband and wife are connected to Him and one another, creating a triangle. Ideally, they are receiving support and strength from God to offer the same to one another in a way they are not able to do without this connection. When the connection between the husband and wife is a solid line (indicating a healthy connection), the children are the beneficiaries of this marital vitality. From the solid horizontal line, we draw vertical lines under it to illustrate each child. This is an illustration of what I call a **T** marriage. The **T** stands for *tethered*. The best definition to describe this word in this context is as follows:

A tether is a cord, fixture, or flexible attachment that characteristically anchors something movable to something fixed; it also may be used to connect two movable objects.

The healthy couple is anchored by God, who is (thankfully) fixed, permanent, the same yesterday, today, and tomorrow. The couple is flexibly attached – two movable objects choosing to be tethered to one another and anchored by God. This tethered line or set of lines is the determining factor of what the children will experience and ultimately imitate in their marriage and parenting efforts.

If the triangle is properly situated and our connection both up and across is solid, whatever is going on between the parents is what's raining down on the children. That is the way it's supposed to go. Get your strength from God, give it to each other, and then it flows down onto the kids naturally. When the marriage is tethered and anchored properly, the children are receiving that sweet rain. They are like little bungee cords able to bounce freely around. They can bounce up toward and down away from their parents without fear because they are also anchored properly by a secure marriage relationship.

There's another version, however, of the marriage-parent focus. It has all of the same players. It has God, husband, wife, and kids; however, the focus is shifted. I call it a **V** marriage. **V** stands for vacated because the marriage tethers have been vacated partially or fully to focus on the children. When this happens, in many cases, the release from the partner also pulls the anchor away from God and attaches it to the parenting role. Why would anyone choose to do this when the first example is so happy and positive all around? This happens in many cases because of that cultural pull to overparent. It's that thought we discussed in chapter 2. It is the pressurized thinking that our kids need to be able to speak four languages, do three sports at one time, and get straight A's, but we aren't supposed to be tired as a result. **V** marriages can result from the fatigue that overparenting produces and the lack of energy remaining for the partner. A **V** marriage can also stem from the need to be anchored in the identity of a 'good parent.' When a parent is overly focused on the kids, it can result from a personal insecurity that plays out as the parent lives through the child. The activities and behaviors of the child become the indicator of the value of the parent.

The main cause of a **V** marriage, however, is an unresolved and chronic conflict between the spouses. (See Diagram on page 29) We illustrate this conflict as a jagged horizontal line between the spouses. When this is the atmosphere in a marriage, it is much easier to turn toward the parent role and toward the children, who more naturally give unconditional love. It is natural to go toward the relationship with the least resistance, and typically, that relationship is with the children. Though parenting is hard, as the adult in the relationship, we are in the power position (see the appendices on the parent roller coaster continuum), which makes the child easier to deal with than a partner with whom you must negotiate and struggle.

We tend to gravitate toward people who love us and help us feel good about ourselves. So, if there is ongoing conflict with your spouse and you have kids, you have a choice. We are conditioned for this choice early on. The warm snuggles, the adoring glances, and the happy smiles children give when they see you are intoxicating. These first bonding experiences make it more natural to focus time and attention on this little one – even as he or she becomes more challenging. The choice is made especially easy if your partner is not quite as appealing or adoring of you. The baby stage lures you in, and if you anchor there, it is a trap for both you and your child.

PARENT OR PARTNER

"T" MARRIAGE

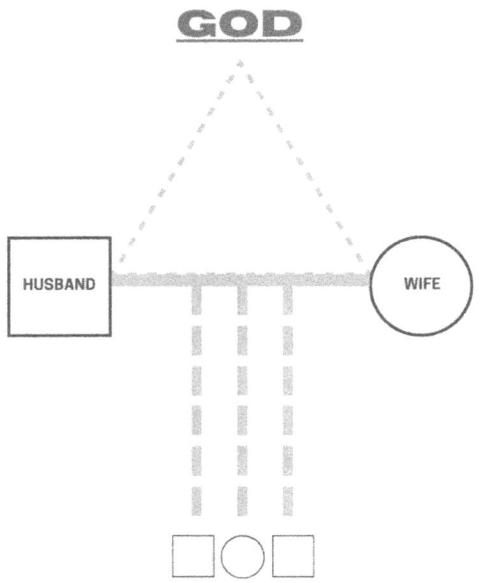

KEY: ☐ - Husband, Father
○ - Wife, Mother
  - Male Child
  - Female Child

TETHERED OR VACATED?

"V" MARRIAGE

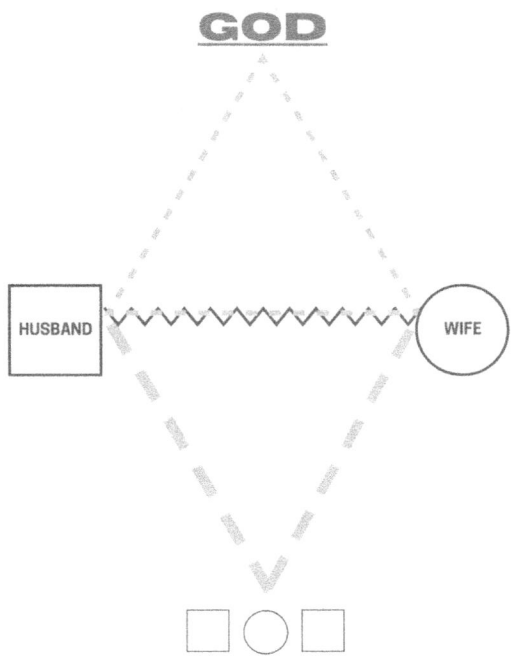

KEY: ☐ - Husband, Father
○ - Wife, Mother
▫ - Male Child
○ - Female Child

BENEFITS OF A T MARRIAGE:

Children benefit from a **T** marriage – in that your relationship is solid, good, and safe. It gives them stability, security, and peace just to be a child. And that's what you want to offer them as best you can. A **T** marriage shows your children how to prioritize and balance these roles. It gives them confidence in marriage and the ability to visualize the same for themselves. **T** marriages teach children what to look for in a marriage partner (Be careful -**V** marriages do this as well!)

OUTCOMES OF A V MARRIAGE:

Parents who overfocus on their kids may think they are giving them the world. Instead, their children are feeling the weight of it. They feel the conflict between their parents and assume responsibility for making things better. They become parentified or over-responsible, and those outcomes have long-standing consequences in every relationship they will have as an adult. This **V** focus is known in psychological terms as triangulation. Triangulation happens when children are pulled into an inappropriate role – one they cannot possibly handle. They learn to carry the feelings and emotions of their parents, and eventually, they will also carry others' feelings and betray their own. Children who are overparented don't feel as secure because the tether between the parents is fractured or vacated. This, in turn, means they are not free to interact with the world as children, free from adult worries and pressures. This anonymous quote says it best,

A child's shoulders were not built to bear the weight of their parent's choices.

So, what are you setting your children up for? Are they getting the benefit of a healthy marriage relationship that results in childhood buoyancy, or are they feeling the weight of the world? Are you setting them up to see someone like me? Many of the people I counsel are operating in their current life based on the faulty beliefs they learned about relationships and themselves from watching their parents and the interpretations they made as children.

The **V** imagery has another disconcerting reference in this chapter. It is a divorce statistic, and it looks like a **V**. At the top of the **V**, after between two to five years of marriage, the divorce rate is high. Divorces, on average, spike after two years of marriage. It dives way down during the next, let's say, 18-22 years. This dive represents the years when the couple is in the thick of parenting; they are dividing and conquering and putting the marriage on hold to stay 'sane.' When do you think the divorce statistic spikes back up? That's right. It spikes again when the kids leave the home, and the couple is left trying to be partners once again without the tie of the parenting role. The marriage fails because there's nothing left between the partners who have operated mostly or solely as parents. Attention to the marriage relationship was lacking in part or absent completely. The partner role was abdicated, and the tethers deteriorated during those *in-between years*. If you have focused on being a *parenting partner,* your marriage will be much less healthy when the kids are gone and may not survive. Being a partner, who *parents* is the better focus. Let's center our conversation on that as we round out toward home!

FIVE
Which Comes Last?

It is not your love that sustains the marriage, but from now on, the marriage that sustains your love.
—*Dietrich Bonhoeffer*

Marriage is our last, best chance to grow up.
—*Joseph Barth*

Let's circle back to the chicken and egg question. The ancient riddle asks which comes *first*. Regarding parent or partner, the more important question may be which comes *last*. Or even better, *which one lasts?* Yes. You'll always be a parent because you have children, and they will always be your little 'eggs,' right? But you will not always be *parenting*. There is a time when you are supposed to stop the active parenting role in favor of an advisory or consultant role. If enough influence is built through healthy relationships, they will want to come back to you as adults for your input – they will know you offer credible and valuable information. Knowing your role on the parenting roller coaster helps you enjoy the ride. (See appendices page 61)

PARENT OR PARTNER

On the contrary, your partnering is meant to be permanent. Marriage is a covenant relationship intended to last 'as long as you both shall live.' Your parenting role, by contrast, is temporary. You are the *temp* parent, filling in for a time with God as the permanent - and perfect - parent. Think about it this way.

You will know your children far longer as adults than you will as children.

So, what type of relationship with them are you setting up for those years after they leave your home? The years from 0-18 go incredibly fast. (For those of you with toddlers, yes, I promise, it goes fast – it just won't seem like it for a while – hang in there!)

With an average life expectancy of 77- 80 years, you could have almost 40 years of an adult-to-adult relationship with your child. Are you ready for that? Are you parenting with the idea that they will be adults, or are you focused on them as children, as *your children?* When we see our children as appendages of us, we cannot see them objectively or parent them for a future without us. You want to be parenting toward life past this little blip of time in favor of the many years you will have with them as adults.

So, who's there in the end? I promise you the kids are going to go, and you will want them to go (some of them more than others). Some will go and come back and then go again. It's important to recognize who is going to be there; who is *supposed* to be there in the end. And if we are going to parent with the end in mind for the best outcome, how about partnering with the end in mind? What if we focus on the relationship we want with our spouse for the rest of our lives? Every marriage and parenting effort will face very real challenges. The tether line will be in conflict at times in every marriage. But does it have to stay this way? The answer is no. If the marriage tethers are vacated, and the focus is on the kids, a longer-lasting problem in your marriage and for the children is created. If your spouse is second, third, or worse, on your priority list or your agenda, your marriage will suffer. Focusing on your kids for 18 years will not leave you with enough relational strength to pull you across the divide of a vacated marriage and back toward one another once they are gone.

There is no holding pattern in marriage. It is a fluid relationship that always moves in one direction or another, either toward friendship and intimacy or away from it. The only thing you must do to drift in your marriage is to do nothing, and it *will* drift because there are so many other things vying for attention. It's got to be a top-of-mind, intentional connection between the partners to avert this movement away from one another.

Yes, I can hear what you may be saying in your head, "Oh, but you don't know *my* spouse!" "He (or she) is impossible to get along with or connect with." "I have tried everything, and nothing works. It's hopeless!" I hear you. You are not crazy; marriage *is* hard – and can seem to be an impossibility. This is especially true when the marriage is based on and tethered insecurely from the start.

There are no perfect marriages. There is also no perfect tether; in fact, some are less effective, and some are downright faulty. Here are a few to avoid; these tethers *will not* hold.

- *The happiness tether*

If a marriage is tethered because of the happiness experienced at the beginning, it will fall apart once unhappiness inevitably comes into the picture.

- *The compatibility tether*

If getting along and understanding one another is the goal, the marriage will unravel as soon as the differences become more prominent, and conflict enters.

- *The healing tether*

When we tether based on feeling deeply known, loved, accepted, supported, valued, or admired, we look to our partner for things they ultimately cannot give. This puts incredible pressure on the marriage. This tether is the one most likely to fail. We often look to our spouse to give us what we are afraid God cannot or will not give. True fulfillment and purpose are only found in God; no person can give what only He can.

This begs the question, "What are healthy tethers that keep a marriage intact?" Here are a few that are crucial to have in place

- *The faith tether*

When a couple is united in their connection to God, they are able to share in the underpinnings of relational health. Base assumptions and philosophies that are grounded in a shared faith are pivotal factors that determine marital outcomes. Human nature dictates that spouses behave in a way to serve each individual rather than serving the couple. People are self-oriented by nature. To love and sacrifice for one another in marriage is not natural beyond the honeymoon phase; it takes a grounding in faith that tells you how to live and love beyond self. It takes a belief in something bigger than the self to behave differently. This is perhaps the most important of all tethers in a marriage. The world, as we discussed earlier, is moving away from honoring marriage as God designed it. This tether is the best (and perhaps only) way to enjoy marriage as intended and raise a family accordingly. Two people who are bound together by God and bonded in marriage through Him are much stronger.

"Though one may be overpowered, two can defend themselves. A cord of three strands is not quickly broken."
Ecclesiastes 4:12

- *The intimacy tether*

Too often, we measure marital success by the absence of conflict. "Okay, we didn't fight, so we are good." That is a good outcome indeed, but a limited perspective. Beyond the absence of conflict, we want to be measuring the presence of intimacy and connection. What are you doing to move toward one another? What's drawing you together? Are you doing what it takes to grow closer or just feeding the status quo? How do we encourage intimacy?

Continue to be curious about your spouse, know what matters to them, and take the time to behave in a way that reflects this. Do the daily, mundane acts that express your awareness of and concern for your spouse. Even conflict, if you do it well, offers the opportunity for greater intimacy. Conflict resolved healthily has been referred to as the *doorway to intimacy*. Though that can sound like a cheesy Hallmark card without much depth, it is an incredibly valuable concept. Conflict in marriage is unavoidable. In reality, if you are having conflict, it means each of you, who were created uniquely, represents those differences. When you go through the conflict together, despite the struggle, you emerge on the other side with greater confidence and optimism about future conflicts. Avoiding conflicts may momentarily keep you 'safe,' though it ultimately puts walls between you creating a lack of intimacy that can kill the relationship.

- *The vision tether*

As the Zig Ziglar saying goes, "If you aim at nothing, you'll hit it every time." Proverbs 29:18 says it this way, *"Without a vision, the people perish."* Vision in marriage is no exception; it is the tether that can keep a couple moving past difficult circumstances and toward shared goals. We discussed the fragility of happiness, compatibility, and healing as tethers. The opposite of those is the vision tether. What keeps the marriage going when those tethers break? When spouses are unhappy and don't feel compatible or healed by one another, the response is often based on the vision for their marriage. What they want it to be and hope it can one day become.

This tether, particularly, has roots in what each person has seen in their parents' marriage—their first vision of marriage. If the marriage they saw as children was healthy, they will have an easier time envisioning their healthy marriage and will be better able to work toward that end. If, however, as is the case for so many, the marriage they witnessed was unhealthy, their vision will be shaped accordingly. This becomes the unconscious stumbling block for many marriages as the couple attempts to find redemption for the pain they experienced in their childhood. Marriage is the place where these experiences and relational settings are reexperienced most closely. It is essential to have a vision for marriage and equally important to assess the vision and where it is rooted objectively. This is where the faith tether is a vital support. Allowing God to help move each spouse to a place of healing will allow their vision for marriage to be less burdened by the history they did not create.

I don't wish to be hyperbolic here, but the next sentence is probably one of the most important things you can ever learn or understand about your partner – it can change everything. Here it is:

Your partner is not the source of your hurt. Neither are they the source of your healing.

Take a moment right now, put the book down, and take that statement in. Write it down for yourself and post it where you can see it often.

PARENT OR PARTNER

Each of you came to the marriage with a set of hurts and habits that predate anything you experience with one another. It's common to say to your spouse; you *make me feel this way*. The truth is that someone or some experience previously made you feel that way. That's why you're sensitive to it with your spouse. It is why you are defensive and easily agitated when he or she *bumps* into it. Find out what *it* is. Until you do, you'll keep circling the same pain points and blaming one another instead of getting over the real reason behind them. (My first book, *Get Over It!* was written for exactly this purpose – to help you identify and move beyond what has you stuck.)

Again, your partner can't heal you. When we put our spouse in the place of God and ask them to heal what hurt us in the past, we will be stuck. **This need places a burden on the spouse that they are unable to carry.** Eventually, that burden can overwhelm the system, and the spouse will pull away from the impossible task. Reread the bolded statement as many times as is necessary to believe it and integrate it into your thinking. Let your spouse off the *healing hook*. Choose to seek help from the True Source. Once you do this, you'll be able to receive from your spouse what they are capable of and responsible for giving, and you'll be more able to give them the same. That's the good stuff. Good for your marriage. Good for your kids.

As a marriage therapist and spouse for 32 years, I can attest that there are days when marriage only works because of a healthy relationship with God. There are days – you know the days – when you cannot see straight from the anger or hurt or betrayal and don't see how you can move on. There may even be times when the tether is ever so thin between you, and the only thing holding you together is the anchor of your faith in God. *That is enough – He is enough.* He promises that His grace is sufficient to meet all our needs. He can and will meet our needs in marriage, but we must focus correctly. First on Him and then on our spouse.

I would encourage you to seek a healthy relationship with God. If you don't have a relationship with God, or if it's more of a religion than a relationship, I hope you will seek that out. A relationship with God will fill in a lot of the gaps for you when you are more than frustrated with your spouse or you don't see eye to eye. Remember, you have an interested party in Him. He is very invested in marriage, in *your* marriage. He is on your side, and He will help you to have the marriage He designed for you – a **T** marriage. (For more information about a relationship with God, see appendices page 51)

To recap, there is no such thing as a perfect marriage, but there is a perfect God who is pro-marriage. He will support and strengthen what He valued as the first recorded act in human history. There will be times when you are not feeling good about one another, and the stress of parenting can undoubtedly intensify the difficulties of the marriage relationship. When a couple feels untethered or insecurely tethered to their spouse, they easily become misaligned in favor of the parenting role. A celebrated and properly focused marriage—not a perfect one—gives your kids everything they need to be healthy adults and have healthy marriages. When we focus first on our partner, we give our children what they need. Remember, whatever happens between the husband and wife in the marriage is the "rain" that comes down on the kids. Focus on making your marriage vibrant and alive - and let the good stuff rain down!

Healthy marriages are the foundation of our society. As the family goes, so goes society. The breakdown of the family has a devastating effect on society. We see what is happening in society based on that breakdown, starting with marriages. You have an opportunity to change things in your marriage, which will change things in your family. The result of this change in your family reaches outward to your neighborhood, then your community, and beyond. Imagine if everyone who reads this book decides to get their focus properly placed first on the marriage and then the kids—what impact that could have on our world!

I hope you have experienced more than an intellectual exercise in reading this book and that you will interact with the concepts in the days to come. May the words jump off the page and encourage you to take application. I pray it becomes a movement ... a *partnering movement* ... *a marriage movement* that blesses the parenting efforts and the children. Let's go after this together. Share this little book and start the conversation!

A PRAYER FOR PARTNERS WHO ARE PARENTS

PARENT OR PARTNER

Thank You that You are the perfect parent. You are Our Father, who has taught us everything we need to know about grace, mercy, and love by the way You love and care for us. We know that children are so important to you. They're your gift. So, it is not that we don't want to focus on them. However, we want to focus on them in the way that benefits them the most. We thank you for the act of marriage and the institution you formed as the priority so that everything flows properly from it.

I pray for every partner who feels alone in their marriage:

You know that pain; come around this partner, Lord. Help him or her to know that they are not alone. You say in Your Word; you will never leave or forsake us. You'll be with us every step of the way and give us everything we need to accomplish what you set before us.

For the partner who's tired, overworked, and overwhelmed:

You tell us to cast our burdens on You, and You will make our yoke light; You care for us. You promise to walk alongside and equip us – to renew our strength when we are weary and can no longer stand. Please give Your strength now to the weary ones.
For the partner who's fearful, Lord:

The stakes are so high, and there is much in this world and in this time to be afraid of, Lord God. You've not given us the spirit of fear. Your Word says you've given us the Spirit of love, power, and sound mind. The enemy's number one tool is fear, and he wants us to live stuck in that fear.

We look to what you tell us in John, and we say thank you that you have told us that we have nothing to fear because you have conquered the world. We are safe in your hands.

For the partner who is confused:

How do I do this? How do I make this shift? Or how do I reach my spouse?
Lord, I thank you that in your Word, you tell us that when we ask for wisdom, you'll give it liberally, not a little bit, not bits and spurts, but liberally. Help us to go to you as the Source. Help us to be transformed by the renewing of our minds. Help us to look back where we need to look back and remove the barriers, the things that we're stuck in that don't allow us to be the mom or dad we want to be, the wife or husband we want to be, the woman or man we want to be.

I pray that everyone has received a word from the Lord today. Something to meet the need they brought in with them. And something they will take home to their families to nourish their spouse and their marriage. Something that will allow their children to receive the sweet rain of a healthy and ordered focus.

PARENT OR PARTNER

Thank you again for Your amazing love. Amen

(from an event held in Miami FL 11/22)

REFERENCES

Kowal, M., Groyecka-Bernard, A., Kochan-Wójcik, M., & Sorokowski, P. (2021). When and how does the number of children affect marital satisfaction? An international survey. PLOS ONE, 16(4), e0249516. https://doi.org/10.1371/journal.pone.0249516

Hirschberger, G., Srivastava, S., Marsh, P., Cowan, C. P., & Cowan, P. A. (2009). Attachment, Marital Satisfaction, and Divorce During the First Fifteen Years of Parenthood. Personal Relationships, 16(3), 401. https://doi.org/10.1111/j.1475-6811.2009.01230.x

Braedehoft, D. J., Mennicke, S. A., Potter, A. M., & Clarke, J. I. (1998) Perceptions attributed by adults to parental overindulgence during childhood. Journal of Family and Consumer Sciences Education, 16(2), 3-17.

PARENT OR PARTNER

Is the Idea of Marriage Dying? | The National Interest, https://nationalinterest.org/blog/buzz/idea-marriage-dying-71451.

10 Questions To Ask Your Husband Every Year | Marriagetrac, https://www.marriagetrac.com/10-questions-ask-husband-every-year/.

161 Best Questions For Married Couples (2023) - Coaching Online, https://www.coaching-online.org/questions-for-married-couples/.

Tether - Wikipedia, https://en.wikipedia.org/wiki/Tether.

APPENDICES

PARENT OR PARTNER

A PRAYER TO RECEIVE JESUS CHRIST AS SAVIOR

The most important relationship for every one of us is our relationship with Jesus Christ. Choosing to believe that he is who he claimed to be—the Son of God and the only way to salvation—and receiving him by faith as your Lord and Savior is the most vital act anyone will ever do. We want life. He is Life. We need cleansing. He is the Living Water. Here is a simple prayer if you have not yet given your life to Jesus and invited him into yours:

Jesus, I believe you are the Son of God, that you died on the cross to rescue me from sin and death and to restore me to the Father. I choose now to turn from my sins, my self-centeredness, and every part of my life that does not please you. I choose you. I give myself to you. I receive your forgiveness and ask you to take your rightful place in my life as my Savior and Lord. Come reign in my heart, fill me with your love and your life, and help me to become a person who is truly loving—a person like you. Restore

PARENT OR PARTNER

me, Jesus. Live in me. Love through me. Thank you, God. In Jesus' name, I pray. Amen.

Wildatheart.org

Help to develop your relationship with God:

Jesus Over Everything by Lisa Whittle
God is Closer Than You Think by John Ortberg
Talking With God by Dick Eastman
At the Table With Jesus by Louie Giglio

MARRIAGE AND PARENTING RESOURCES

PARENT OR PARTNER

10 QUESTIONS TO ASK YOUR HUSBAND EACH YEAR

1. *What are you enjoying most about our relationship right now?* Talking about what is going right will create optimism and renew energy. Tell him what you enjoy most about him.

2. *What has been your biggest surprise in the last year?* This is a great way to gain insight into his expectations and the things he considers most important.

3. *Where would you like our relationship to be this time next year?* It doesn't matter where you are, there's always room to be better. He might say, "I'd like to see more spontaneous intimacy," or, "I want us to be moving forward together in our faith." He could say, "I want our relationship to involve

more fun!"

4. *How are you feeling about life in general?* Never assume you know how your husband is feeling. He may look okay on the surface but be overwhelmed underneath. Don't just listen to what he says but be sure to read between the lines as well.

5. *What are your dreams for our future?* If you want to know what gets him up in the mornings and what gives him hope, it's going to be this one. Find out his highest hopes for your future together. Give him the time to paint the picture for you.

6. *If you could go anywhere, where would you go?* Encourage him to fantasize about his ideal vacation. Get excited and dream with him. Maybe someday you can surprise him and make it a reality.

7. *How do you think we're doing financially?* This needs to be an ongoing conversation. Just like a board of directors of a business meets annually to evaluate the finances and the plan for the coming year, a husband and wife should

do the same.

8. *What do you want to do this year to improve your health?* Being in shape and eating well gives you more energy in everyday life. Encourage one another to exercise. It is a great activity to do together. Explore creative cooking and focus on food that makes you feel good.

9. *What is one thing you would change about how our family relates to one another?* This is one to brainstorm together. Set a vision of what a healthy family looks like, then model it. A few examples could be less TV, more constructive communication with less yelling, getting time away together, or eating dinner together more .

10. *What is one thing I give my time to that you think would be better spent elsewhere?* You need to know where he wants your time. This will give him an open door to ask for it. It's an opportunity to see what he thinks is important.

PARENT OR PARTNER

QUESTIONS FOR COUPLES

- How am I doing as a husband/wife in general?
- What are you most excited about in our relationship during this season?
- If you could see two things change about me, what would they be?
- In what ways can I honor you more?
- What are your biggest fears about our relationship?
- As a husband/wife, how can I show more love/sensitivity to you?
- Are you dealing with anything that I can help you with currently?
- How can we improve our intimacy or take it to the next level?
- What's your dream date night or weekend with me?
- If you had three wishes to wish for our future, what would they be?
- What are a few ways I need to be more understanding?
- What are a few ways you desire to see our finances improve?
- What are three places within 200 miles where you would

like to spend a few days?
- What strengths do I bring to our relationship?
- In what ways can I improve as a husband/wife?
- What are your top three favorite love songs, and why?
- Do you feel more emotionally connected than you did early in our relationship?
- What are two things we forgot to celebrate this year?
- What were some things we used to do before we were married that you miss now?
- What do I need to know most about you right now?
- What have you learned to appreciate about me that you did not know when we were first married?
- Are you satisfied with the amount of time we spend together?
- Do I tell you I love you enough?
- In what ways can we build our friendship more?

PARENTING RESPONSIBILITY ROLLER COASTER
Know your Role, Enjoy the Ride

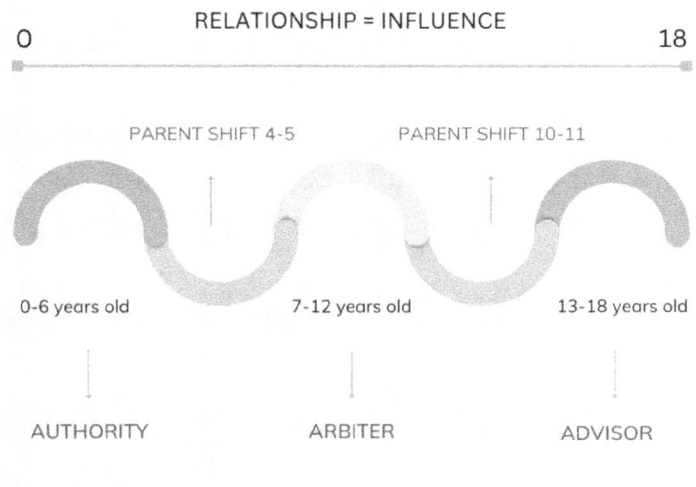

Sally Livingston, LMFT

PARENT OR PARTNER

ROADMAP TO RAISING MY ADULT

List below the traits you would like to "seed" into your child as they enter adulthood. (ie. honesty, compassion, generosity, faith)

-
-
-
-
-
-
-
-
-

Use this as a template to guide you as you go - what are the daily seeds to plant, what needs to be watered, and what is to be weeded to grow my adult?

MARRIAGE AND PARENTING QUOTES:

PARENT OR PARTNER

MARRIAGE AND PARENTING QUOTES:

What counts in making a happy marriage is not so much how compatible you are but how you deal with incompatibility.
Leo Tolstoy

Many marriages would be better if the husband and the wife clearly understood that they are on the same side.
Zig Ziglar

A happy marriage is the union of two good forgivers.
Ruth Graham

Train up a child in the way he should go but make sure you go that way yourself.
Charles Spurgeon

It is far easier to shape a child than to repair an adult.
Dr. Tony Evans

Childhood is a short season.
Helen Hayes

Your children are the greatest gift God will give to you, and their souls the heaviest responsibility He will place in your hands. Take time with them, teach them to have faith in God. Be a person in whom they can have faith. When you are old, nothing else you've done will have mattered as much.
Lisa Wingate

Children learn more from what you are than what you teach.
W. E. Du Bois

Instead of solving your kid's problems, teach them how to think: biblically, logically, and emotionally.
Lysa Terkeurst

Each day of our lives we make deposits in the memory banks of our children.
Chuck Swindoll

AUTHOR BIO

PARENT OR PARTNER

Sally was born in Miami, Florida, as Sally Snow White. Though the name is legitimate (named after 2 grandmothers) she is fond of the fairy tale. She has been a Licensed Marriage and Family Therapist, church ministry leader and parent educator for almost 30 years. She has worked with many people caught in the trap of believing they have to simply survive what they were given or experienced as a child. She loves counseling, speaking, teaching, and helping people move to a place of freedom that only comes by accepting God's Truth about who they are and where they can go in life. Sally works to move people from where they are to where they want to be with grace and purpose through her business *Life to the Full*. Sally and her husband, Scott – a retired Fire Captain – live in Florida and have three amazing adult children, two amazing children-in-law, and two incredible grandsons.

More about Sally:
BA in Psychology from Baylor University
MS in Marriage and Family Therapy from St. Thomas University
Licensed in the State of Florida (LMFT), Licensed in the State of North Carolina (LMFT)
Licensed to Ministry
Church/Business Consulting (Lifegauge Solutions)
Certified RightPath Trainer
Prepare/Enrich Certified Facilitator
YouVersion Bible App Reading Plan Contributor
Published Author:
> *Get Over It!: 4 Steps to Breaking Free from the Stuck Cycle in 2019*

AUTHOR BIO

Get Over It! Bible Study Guide

COMING SOON

ALSO BY SALLY LIVINGSTON

BUY BOOK NOW!

Get OVER It! Amazon Best Seller!
4 Steps to Breaking Free
from the Stuck Cycle

BUY STUDY GUIDE NOW!

Get OVER IT & live Life to the full
Great for Churches & Small Group
Bible Studies

TESTIMONIAL

"Sally is a gifted speaker. If you are looking for someone to lead marriage and family events, staff development, or care ministry formation, please let me commend her to you."
Mark Lesher, Executive Pastor (retired), Christ Journey Church

"Sally has a poised approach which brings confidence to any group she partners with. She makes organizations and relationships stronger."
Lilibeth Garcia, Founder, The Legacy Ministries

"Sally brought my wife and I 'home.' The tools she shared with us helped return our relationship to the beautiful, supportive, and loving place it had once been.
M & C, a married couple

www.ingramcontent.com/pod-product-compliance
Lightning Source LLC
Chambersburg PA
CBHW050208130526
44590CB00043B/3303